STOP
PROCRASTINATING
IN SIX STEPS

Get Back on Track With Six Powerful
Productivity Strategies for Success

Other books by Gemma Ray

2018 - Self Discipline: A How-To Guide to Stop Procrastination and Achieve Your Goals in 10 Steps

2020 - Stop Procrastinating and Start Living: Beat Procrastination and Boost Productivity for Self Care and Success

ISBN 9798531112859

www.gemmaray.com

For my friend, Leah Bramich, who moaned that she didn't have time to procrastinate by reading a full book on procrastination. You were the inspiration for writing this mini version!

Contents

More than Just a Mini Book

I know how difficult it is to make and maintain changes in your life. Discipline is really tough for many of us! I wanted to create additional tools that would help you to understand and improve your own relationship with self-discipline, so I would love to offer you a gift as a valued reader.

Special offer! FREE Online Goal setting Masterclass & Workbook
To accompany this book, I have created a powerful Goal Setting Masterclass and workbook. Designed to help you get clarity on your goals, shine a light on what's been holding you back and eradicate procrastination once and for all.

Get your free gifts at **www.gemmaray.com/bonus**

Procrastination Busting Starts Here...

Thank you for downloading this eBook which aims to help you go from procrastination panic to diligently disciplined in six steps.

I'm Gemma Ray, author of the Amazon #1 best sellers Self-Discipline, a How-to Guide to Stop Procrastination & Achieve Your Goals and Stop Procrastinating and Start Living. I have successfully learned how to overcome procrastination and developed self-discipline in my life and the lives of others.

I'm not someone who is ex-military or likes to do discipline with aggression. I teach discipline and procrastination busting methods to real people with real jobs, real families, real commitments and real lives.I believe there is no such thing as being lazy. Research suggests we procrastinate because one or more of our basic needs are not being met.I have created this mini book as the perfect thing for you to procrastinate on! This isn't as long as my published books, is easy to read in one sitting and contains easy to action hints, tips and hacks you can put into practice straight away. It is the foolproof system of pressing an imaginary panic button when procrastination teeters on the verge of endangering your discipline.

Procrastination has the power to destroy your mood, add to your stress, make you feel like a failure and get you into trouble.

A better, brighter you can emerge on the other side of overwhelm and these foolproof strategies could be the key to achieving your goals.

Need some extra help? Check out **www.gemmaray.com** for more productivity resources.

Step 1

Prepare to Fail & Forgive the Failure

Yes, that's right, I said prepare to fail. If you're reading this eBook the chances are you're someone who is already struggling with procrastination. It affects all of us! Even that super-human colleague of yours or that focused friend who always seems to have their life together.

So what do I mean by preparing to fail? Well, first of all we start with something really important.

FORGIVENESS

Scientific studies have proven that procrastination is linked to feelings of shame. When we start to work on our procrastination tendencies, we should start with forgiveness of the self. It does not matter what has happened in the past, you cannot change what has already happened. You only have today onwards. So draw a line under what has happened in the past with procrastination and get ready to move on. If you'd like to read up on this further, look up the Carlton University study titled *I Forgive Myself, Now I Can Study: How self-forgiveness for procrastinating can reduce future procrastination.*

I want to help you through a process of self-forgiveness through the following journal prompts. Writing things down helps you to process your thoughts. If you are not a fan of journaling, you could use these prompts as a talking point with a trusted friend, relative or coworker.

Write down the tasks that you tend to procrastinate on the most. Think about the things you put off that cause you the most stress.

_____

_____

_____

_____

_____

_____

_____

_____

Thinking about those tasks you procrastinate on the most, how can you forgive yourself for not always getting them done?

_____

_____

_____

Now complete this sentence:

I forgive myself for _____ *[task you procrastinate on]* I cannot change what has happened in the past, but I can look to the future which is within my control.

Please take a moment to really feel into that self-forgiveness. It is very important to let go of what has been and that you cannot change. Allowing yourself a moment of self-forgiveness will help you start with a fresh new perspective.

The second part of this first tip is to:

PREPARE TO FAIL

That's right! You need to set up a strategy for the NEXT time you get caught out by the pain of procrastination.

Have you ever trained in First Aid? The art of administering CPR or treating a burn or dealing with a fracture is covered in a course so you know what to do in the event of an emergency.

This comparison is a little dramatic but I want you to think about creating a First Aid strategy for the next time procrastination hits.

The first thing to do is identify the signs you're about to enter a procrastination wormhole. Procrastination is often our response to stress, fear, overwhelm and is NOT necessarily laziness.

Many people get angry with themselves when procrastination strikes. They feel like they've let themselves down. They feel like they've failed. They feel like they can't trust themselves.

These are all normal emotional responses to the effects and consequences of procrastination. So in order to undo this emotional response to overwhelm and stress, we need to be prepared for how procrastination starts in the first place.

So let's get to know you and your behaviours a little better in this eBook. Use a notepad or journal to answer some of the exercises.

What Do You Procrastinate on Most and Why Is It Important?

Are there specific tasks in your life that you always struggle to feel motivated to do?

Taking the list you have written from question 1, I want you to identify three main tasks that you always seem to put off. We are going to examine why each one is important. What does it mean if you get these tasks done? More money, more organised? Less stress down the line? Someone else's happiness?

You might want to use this format:

I procrastinate on (task #1)

Getting task #1 completed is important to me because:

_____

_____

_____

I procrastinate on (task #2)

_____

Getting task #2 completed is important to me because:

_____

_____

_____

I procrastinate on (task #3)

_____

Getting task #3 completed is important to me because:

_____

_____

_____

Identify Your Procrastination Warning Signs

Outline key things you 'do' 'say' or 'think' when you can feel the prickle of procrastination about to take over you.

It might be that you comfort eat. You might think it wise to suddenly start binge watching a Netflix series. You might bury yourself in your phone.

Have a really good think about your own patterns.

When you're really avoiding tasks, what do you tend to do instead?

_____

_____

_____

What patterns of behaviour do you present?

_____

_____

_____

Are there any patterns to you acting like this?

_____

_____

_____

What distracts you?

_____

_____

_____

What do you need to do less of in these scenarios?

_____

_____

_____

What usually gets you motivated to start? (Or do you panic at the last moment?)

_____

_____

_____

Keep these behaviours that you have outlined in mind. We will revisit them later in this eBook.

Step 2

Prepare the Right Environment

Your environment is everything! Getting in the right environment free of distractions that can derail you makes tasks much easier.

If you work in an open plan office then it's likely you will be distracted by colleagues many times throughout the day.

- Could you book a private meeting room to help you focus?

- If you work from home, where do you work from?

- Do you have a dedicated space? Is it clean and tidy?

- Does it light you up and make you feel good?

I know tidying a desk is a common example of procrastination but there's scientific research about the need for things to be in order before you can focus. So if you need to tidy your desk, get it done but set a strict timer.

Environment Exercise

I want you to think about something you procrastinate on a regular basis or a task that is pressing that you can't seem to get started or motivated to do. Something that you just always put off starting or doing.

What is your environment like when you're trying to attempt this task? Describe it, or even better go to that place now when answering these questions.

_____

_____

_____

What are the positives in this environment?

_____

_____

_____

What are the negatives? Who or what distracts you?

_____

_____

_____

Now think about being more productive in this particular environment, what would create the optimum condition here to complete this task?

(Describe it in as much detail as possible - how are you going to work best?)

_____

_____

_____

Have a good think about your environment around those irritating tasks you put off. There will usually be a way you can make the environment work better for you and put you in the right frame of mind to tackle your tasks. Which leads nicely onto...

Step 3

Get in the Right Frame of Mind

Are you mentally prepped and ready to kick procrastination's butt?

If you're in a state of stress, upset, discomfort or overwhelm it is time to regain some mental toughness and get your mind prepared to win.

Deep Breathing Techniques

If you've been feeling overwhelmed and stressed out, working on your breathing can be a great starting point.

There are many meditation tracks on YouTube that can help you get in the zone with your breathing techniques. You may have also heard of Wim Hof? If not, Google him and his specialist breathing techniques that many people swear by to set them up for the day. He has an app called WHM that is really good.

Music Anchoring

Have you ever seen the beginning of a boxing match? What do the fighters do? They come into the ring to a specific predetermined piece of music that means something to them. It's the music that gets them fired up and ready in their winning mentality.

Music has a great power to change our conscious emotive state. There will be songs in your life that instantly take you back to a moment in time, a memory or a person. If you don't already have a piece of music, think of a song that is going to be YOUR anti-procrastination track. It's going to be your song that you come into the ring with and knock out procrastination in one punch.

You could use this track on your way to work in the car, on your way to the gym, on your running playlist or even just play it at your desk through your headphones when you're about to start that important piece of work.

What is your ultimate favourite feelgood track that could get you in the zone?

Bonus exercise: if you have more than one track that uplifts you and makes you feel motivated then why not create a digital playlist on your streaming service of choice. Create your GSD (Get Stuff Done) playlist to help you get in the mood, the frame of mind and motivate you into action.

The Five Second Rule

International speaker and best selling author Mel Robbins became famous using her 5 Second Rule technique. It's pretty simple, and the idea was inspired by a rocket launch she watched on TV.

5...4...3...2...1...lift off!

Mel realised that her own procrastination could be overcome using this same technique. 5,4,3,2,1 and action! Getting yourself in the right frame of mind might include the 5 second rule before you start work. 5...4...3...2...1 - START! It could be your mental mantra to get you out of procrastination and into being productive.

Switch Off and Remove Distractions

Did you know? It takes around 23 minutes once distracted to go back to a task. So every time a notification pops up on your phone or a coworker interrupts you at your desk or that email pings into your inbox, what happens? You get distracted. And then it's 23 minutes to get back in the zone. Is it any wonder we all procrastinate?!

Headphones are a great way to switch off, whether you choose to play any music out of them or not! Wearing headphones in work instantly tells your colleagues you're working and focused and don't want to be distracted.

Personally, I can't have too much music in the background while I am working. Anything with words and a vocal distracts me so I tend to listen to classical music while writing or I do use binaural beats which I highly recommend. Binaural beats are sound waves played at specific frequencies. The frequencies are meant to enhance the tasks you are doing such as writing, resting, problem solving. Type 'binaural beats' into your app store of choice and have a play with the apps out there. I highly recommend a Binaural Beat soundtrack or audio programme for focused work.

Remove distractions if you need to focus, including:

- Turn your phone off
- If you can't turn your phone off, turn off your phone notifications temporarily
- Switch off your email programme
- Turn off your office phone
- Book out a meeting room or quiet space if you have noisy colleagues
- Ask to work from home if this environment works for you

Is there anything else you could do to get in the right frame of mind? Make a note of it here:

_____

_____

_____

_____

_____

Step 4

Use a Timer to Get Realistic and Focused With Your Productivity

Do you actually know the average time your most procrastinated-on tasks take you? I bet you'd be shocked! This is a great exercise you can do today to help the next time you find yourself procrastinating. I advise this exercise for everyone who finds themselves putting things off.

Start to time everything in your life. Do it over the course of a couple of days or a week and make a list. I get my clients to do this and it completely changes the way they work. It is the one thing that helps time management, organising your diary and overcoming procrastination when it feels like overwhelm.

Time everyday tasks in your life and business. Prioritise auditing the tasks you tend to procrastinate on the most. The very first time I did this exercise and when I get clients to do this, I advise the following:

- Set the digital timer going on your phone
- Turn the phone over so the screen faces down (and doesn't distract you)
- Work as your usual speed on the different tasks you are tracking

When I first did this exercise I was working full-time as a done-for-you copywriter. I was procrastinating on a lot of client work which meant I would then panic, do it all late at night, not rest properly and always feel like I was chasing my tail and doing a crap job. I'd sometimes look at my schedule and wonder how the heck I could fit all my work in, causing overwhelm, Yet I'd find myself on my phone instead of working just making the problem a lot worse.

I realised that the average long form social media post takes me 8 minutes to write. So when a client wants me to write 30 posts I know that I need 4 hours to complete this. I worked out that the average 3 minute client video takes 5 hours to edit. It takes me 45 minutes to write a newsletter and depending on the length of the award entry, it takes around 6 hours to complete an award application.

Once I had these lists and lists of times that tasks take me, it helped me be more realistic in planning my time. Rather than looking at my watch thinking "I don't have time to write this right now" and overthink it, I could be realistic and think "Yes, I've got an hour let's see if I can get it done." Because attempting SOMETHING was better than not getting started at all.

When I timed my regular work tasks it really did change my life. It became a game. Me against the clock and I was able to get realistic with my workload. I was able to work smarter and more efficiently but I was also able to say no to things that I knew I didn't have time for.

I'd urge you to do the same and time all those tasks you procrastinate on.

Do this with as many tasks as you can that you tend to put off and have a more realistic picture of how long things take. You won't feel as overwhelmed next time you look at that long to-do list.

You'll be in a position where you can really plan your tasks ahead with the time you have available and you'll also feel more empowered to say a firm "no" to those things you know you won't have time for.

My main recurring tasks at work are: *Time*

_____   _____

_____   _____

_____   _____

_____   _____

My main recurring tasks at home are: *Time*

_____   _____

_____   _____

_____   _____

_____   _____

The Pomodoro Technique

There's another way to use a timer that will help you feel more focused, productive and help stop overwhelm when you're working.

Did your grandma or anyone in the family ever have a mechanical kitchen timer?? Well if you've seen these before, chances are you've used them for timing boiled eggs or that chicken in the oven. I love to use one of these tomato timers for a productive way of working called The Pomodoro Technique.

Francesco Cirillo found that in his college years he wasn't using his study time well and would get distracted. So he grabbed his tomato shaped kitchen timer and developed the Pomodoro Technique which has now been adopted by millions of people looking to focus and knuckle down on their tasks.

The Pomodoro Technique involves breaking down tasks into 25 minute chunks of time. The idea is that you work for 25 focused minutes on ONE TASK and that one task only, and then take a 5 minute break.

After four consecutive working time blocks, you take a longer break, around 20 or 30 minutes.

Pomodoro 1	10:00	Write blog
Break	10:25	Make a coffee
Pomodoro 2	10:30	Format blog and post it
Break	10:55	Check social media

I also recommend having this tomato timer or grabbing an inexpensive mechanical timer so you always have it to hand. Yes, you can use digital options or the timer on your phone, but I found these far too easy to override. A mechanical timer was one of the best things I ever invested in to keep me on track and focused in my work.

I have a free Pomodoro PDF tracker you can download and use if you'd like to try this method.

Go to **gemmaray.com/pomodoro** to get your free digital Pomodoro planner.

Step 5

Stay Accountable

Have you ever had a partner on something to do with work or training? Maybe you've had a gym buddy or diet buddy in the past? Perhaps you've had a proper accountability buddy or a coach?

Staying accountable really helps you to eradicate procrastination. Depending on your accountability style, most people benefit from having someone to check in with and remain accountable to.

According to a study by the Association for Talent Development, you're 95% more likely to stick to a goal if you have someone to stay accountable to.

Ways to Stay Accountable

If you struggle with procrastination in particular, then accountability around getting started on tasks is usually a positive exercise.

Get an Accountability Buddy

Is there someone who you can check in with regularly, whether that is a professional coach or mentor who you pay, or simply a friend or colleague? This person needs to be someone you trust and most definitely someone who will not trigger you. You need to think of someone who will be very supportive.

Agree on a set of actions with your accountability buddy and check-in at regular intervals on the tasks you achieve, as you tick them off your to-do list. If you haven't achieved them, be honest and work together on being more realistic in your actions to get your tasks completed.

You could also hire a professional accountability mentor (like me!) who will have systematic methods and processes to help you stick to your weekly actions.

Who could you connect with to help you stay accountable?

_____

_____

_____

Start a Blog

When I speak of starting a 'blog', this doesn't necessarily have to be on a blogging platform. A lot of people might get scared of the prospect of sorting out the tech and investment needed for a blogging website. Instead, people keep it simple and inexpensive by starting their 'blog' on social media. I know that technically this isn't a proper blog in the traditional sense, but just getting down your thoughts and feelings as you move through your journey can be beneficial. It doesn't matter which platform you choose, putting your action steps out there to the world and using your writing on social media or a blogging platform can keep you accountable. Plenty of people start dedicated Instagram profiles or just post on their social media to stay accountable. If you wanted to start your own proper blog with your own website, that is a possibility too. Just remember the time it will take to keep it going. You don't want to add another task into the mix if you are already overwhelmed!

One of the simplest ways to stay accountable using social media is to post your daily actions and then report back on them. At the time of writing, I have been doing this myself for around six months now, and I love my daily 'Ta Dah' lists on my Instagram stories. You can follow me here **www.instagram.com/gemmadeeray**, and you'll see the daily lists I post. If you'd like a copy of the Instagram story templates to use yourself, you can download them for free here: **www.gemmaray.com/instatemplates**. I would love for you to tag me into your stories so I can see what you're getting up to.

Start a WhatsApp or Facebook Group

If you're on a mission and working towards a sporting endeavour or weight loss, why not round up a few like-minded friends and create a dedicated group where you all keep one another accountable?

You can post your daily progress in the group and help inspire each other on. I am part of a running group, and there is nothing more motivating than a sea of Strava maps and run times to make you want to lace up your trainers. I also have a group with friends who are on a fitness mission and their recipes and healthy food inspiration on WhatsApp is very inspirational and gives me lots of ideas for new recipes.

Hire a Coach

If you really need the help and dedicated support, consider hiring a coach. If you are struggling with procrastination in your day to day work, you may want to look into a business coach or mentor. If it is your health and fitness that is the priority you just can't seem to prioritise then consider hiring a nutritionist, personal trainer or online well-being coach.

There are coaches for every sector and challenge that you may have. I work as an accountability mentor and a communications coach. I love to help people stick to their action steps to achieve their goals, and I adore helping business owners to get clear with their communications so they can market and grow their business.

Join a Group

There are so many groups on social media platforms like Facebook and LinkedIn that could help keep you accountable. Whether it's fitness, business or even more niche subjects related to your hobbies, if you search for it, there will be a group on it!

You might also wish to join a group in person, like a running or sporting group. The community element of the group acts as brilliant accountability to keep you wanting to return and participate in more events.

After reading this chapter, spend a few minutes outlining ways in which you could be accountable to achieve your goals. Think about the people you could ask for help or the groups you could join. What or who could help you achieve your goals quicker?

Step 6

Drop Perfectionism

Ahhh perfectionism is an absolute nightmare, isn't it? Most of us perfectionists don't even admit we are a perfectionist. If you've ever waited for the right moment, if you've ever worried about other people's criticism of your actions or if you've always been afraid of making mistakes then chances are you're a perfectionist.

Research suggests that perfectionism can be closely related to depression and self-esteem. It makes sense if you think about it. If we believe negative things about ourselves and we tell ourselves that we aren't good enough, then we will struggle to accept that our actions and the work or outcomes we produce are good enough.

But who decides what is actually good enough? Surely doing SOMETHING and it not being absolutely perfect is better than doing nothing at all?

There are a few different types of perfectionists, but we usually fall into these common categories:

- The "I'll do it soon" perfectionist. This is the one that never starts. The one who desperately wants to achieve something but immediately starts doubting themselves and thinks they can't do it. They don't even start, and they don't even try.

- The "My standards are too high" perfectionist. This perfectionist makes a start, sets a goal but sets the goal so high that they always fail. They work hard, sometimes too hard, but never seem to appreciate what they have achieved or celebrate their successes. This person might also want everything to be perfect before they take action. They think they need to exercise every day to lose weight, set a goal to write an unrealistic number of words to get the book finished or set impossible run distances to tackle in a month.

I used those examples above because they are my previous examples and where I failed. If things were not perfect, I would throw the towel in too quickly.

Personally, I've found that stripping goals back into the tiniest of actions is the way to overcome perfectionism. When I think too far in advance of the big goal and what I want to achieve, I immediately think I'm not good enough, and I'm paralysed by procrastination.

In his book Atomic Habits, James Clear states that every new habit should start with a two-minute action. This is about mastering the habit of showing up, not about doing things perfectly.

He states that you can break down any major goal into one simple, straightforward action that should not take more than two minutes. For example, "Run three miles" becomes "Tie my running shoes" or one that I have found really useful is stop saying "Write 2,000 words" and instead say "Open my manuscript". If you start with the smallest action, complete it, get used to winning and master how it feels, you will naturally start to add more to your actions.

- So running a marathon is **extremely hard**

- Running a 5k is **hard**

- Walking 10,000 steps daily is **moderately difficult**

- Walking 10 minutes is **easy**

- Tying your running shoes is **very easy**

Using my example of writing a book, you could use the scale above

- Launching a best-selling book is **extremely hard**

- Editing a book is **hard**

- Writing a book is moderately **difficult**

- Writing a chapter is **easy**

- Opening your manuscript is **very easy**

Could you use the same scale for anything you regularly procrastinate on?

What new habits do you want to form that you could start off with only a two-minute action or decide on an action step with significantly less expectation than achieving your goal in one session?

Learn to Surrender

Dropping perfectionism also requires a sense of surrender. You really have to let go of that need for everything to be perfect.

- There will never be a perfect time

- There will never be perfect circumstances

- Anything you produce will never be 100% perfect

To overcome perfectionism, focus on getting things DONE, not getting things perfect. So using all the strategies outlined in this book, could you just work on getting things done?

Could you set a timer to see how long things take to get done and once done, accept they are done? (No tweaking, changing and fiddling later).

Could you use the Pomodoro timer to break your tasks into 25 minutes of focused action and see how you get on?

Could you accept that the environment you are in will never be perfect so instead work on making it as best as it can be? Remember - remove distractions, get that winning song on, get fired up!

But, above all can you truly accept that things will never ever be 100% perfect? When you focus on done over perfect, when you are regularly getting things done, over and over again, you will eventually feel empowered to tackle your tasks with ease. There is a wonderful phrase I want you to write on your mirrors, on post-it notes in the car or your desk, on every journal or notebook:

"I am enough."

Remind yourself of this every time you feel the paralysing effects of perfectionism and try with all of your might to just take that first step. A blank document cannot be edited. You cannot run a marathon without taking that first step. Your book will not write itself. You ARE enough, and your efforts are enough. So take action and see where your action steps take you.

After reading this chapter, think about your relationship with perfectionism.

What goals have you put on hold or been stuck with perfectionism procrastination paralysis because things aren't 'perfect'?

_____

_____

_____

_____

_____

_____

_____

_____

Where have you been getting overwhelmed thinking your goals are too big and scary, so you've not taken any action?

_____

_____

_____

_____

_____

_____

_____

_____

_____

_____

Where can you cut yourself some slack and take your goals back to basics?

_____

_____

_____

_____

_____

_____

_____

_____

_____

_____

What are the smallest and tiniest action steps you can commit to that will get you moving towards achieving your biggest and most important goals?

In Summary

It's really easy for me to say "Just try these action steps!" to stop procrastinating. When you're in that mindset, it is super difficult to break! Pushing the procrastination panic button requires you to create some forward-thinking strategies.

When you know the signs of your own procrastination, and when you've developed a strategy to combat it, it gets easier to overcome each time.

That's why I believe learning about yourself, asking yourself questions about your own fears and exploring why things are important to you is the key to start to train your brain to reduce your procrastination time gradually.

If you really are struggling with procrastination, then I have a number of free downloads available via my website at **www.gemmaray.com** You may also choose to join my FREE Level:Up Facebook community where we support one another with all aspects of productivity and goal achievement to level up in all areas of our lives. To join the group, please click here at **bit.do/levelupfacebookgroup**. Don't forget to answer the questions and agree to the rules first.

90 Day Accountability Programme – Change Your Life One Decision at a Time!

If you know you need a little more support to get inspired into action, I run a paid 90-day programme three times per year. Entry to the group is by application only to ensure you are the right fit for the group. We operate as a tight-knit structured and focused group of people who all help to achieve goals and support one another. To apply for the next 90-day programme, please email gemma@gemmaray.com to find out the latest dates and availability.

Space for Additional Notes and Learnings

About Gemma Ray

Gemma Ray should have a PhD in procrastination. Her book on self-discipline (that she had no self-discipline to write) continues to top the bestseller charts.

Her second book Stop Procrastinating and Start Living was a runaway success gaining bestseller status and the #1 spot in over 20 categories in UK and US Amazon bookstores.

Gemma writes from the heart for real people who need a hand pulling their finger out to take action and level up all areas of their life. She has written for a number of publications, newspapers, blogs and businesses before realising a childhood dream of becoming an author. She writes "the books I need to read myself" and packages her research in a personal, fun account that is easy to read and even easier to implement.

Self-proclaiming to "Not always having all my s*** together", Gemma's down-to-earth delivery and style makes you feel like you have a friend between the pages giving you simple advice over a coffee. She continues that support for her readers through her 1:1 private accountability mentoring, online coaching courses and social media channels, giving readers direct access to her no-nonsense witty retorts that makes accountability a whole lot of fun.

Gemma is a radio presenter, best selling author, content marketing and PR specialist and always the most filthy person in a WhatsApp group chat. She should probably establish the first chapter of Oversharers Anonymous, is the world's worst cook and the clumsiest person you'll ever meet.

Catch Gemma co-hosting both the Honest to Gob podcast and Body Smart podcast. Search your favourite podcast platform.

Follow her on Instagram **@gemmadeeray**

facebook.com/GemmaRayPullYourfingerOut

Printed in Great Britain
by Amazon

39604608R00030